UNCOMMON WOMEN AND OTHERS

BY
WENDY WASSERSTEIN

★

DRAMATISTS
PLAY SERVICE
INC.

2

To my brothers,

Abner and Bruce

UNCOMMON WOMEN AND OTHERS was presented by The Phoenix Theatre at the Marymount Manhattan Theatre, in New York City, on November 21, 1977. It was directed by Steven Robman; the scenery and lighting were by James Tilton; and the costumes were by Jennifer von Mayrhauser. The cast, in order of appearance, was as follows:

KATE QUIN	Jill Eikenberry
SAMANTHA STEWART	Ann McDonough
HOLLY KAPLAN	Alma Cuervo
MUFFET DI NICOLA	Ellen Parker
RITA ALTABEL	Swoosie Kurtz
MRS. PLUMM	Josephine Nichols
SUSIE FRIEND	Cynthia Herman
CARTER	Anna Levine
LEILAH	Glenn Close

CHARACTERS

In the present:

KATE QUIN
SAMANTHA STEWART
MUFFET DI NICOLA
HOLLY KAPLAN
RITA ALTABEL

At the college:

MRS. PLUMM
SUSIE FRIEND
CARTER, a catatonic
LEILAH

SETTING

A restaurant in the present, and six years earlier at a college for women.

NOTE ON THE SETTING

The present, 1978, in a restaurant, and six years earlier at a college for women. In the present the women are around 27 years old.

The play should be played on a single playing area. In other words the restaurant in the present becomes the college living room. This will give continuity to the episodic nature of the play. Also, the play is really a memory play and this should be made clear. The benches indicated in the scene design area are also used as lounges or beds for the girls. I would try to keep it simple and use pastel colors that would fit both a ladies restaurant and a women's college.

As far as costumes, the girls should be wearing what they first wore in the restaurant. However, slight alterations and additions could take place in the past, like sweaters or Rita's cap. The characters who enter at the college, however, should be dressed for that particular period. Finally, Holly should wear her raccoon coat to the restaurant.

CHARACTERS

MUFFET DI NICOLA: An attractive woman, wry and cheerful. Muffet is stylish and attractive to men. Her friends would agree that she has charm. Muffet's intelligence is quick, but she never dotes on it. As Muffet approaches thirty she is re-examining her younger tenets that men were just more interesting than women and life would simply fall into place. This examination is not always evident in her behavior because it is just beginning. And anyway, Muffet remains charming, especially to men.

HOLLY KAPLAN: Hair disheveled, yet well cut. She wears expensive clothes that don't quite match, not because she doesn't know what matches, but because she doesn't want to try too hard. That would be too embarrassing. A relier for many years on the adage, "If she lost twenty pounds, she'd be a very pretty girl, and if she worked, she'd do very well.'" Holly alternates between being a spectator and a spectacle. She has devised a strong moral code of warmth to those you love and wit to those you're scared of. Holly saw the Radio City Easter Show in Second Grade and planned to covert.

KATE QUIN: In business suit, holding an attaché case that she is quite aware of. The attaché case alternately makes her feel like a successful grown-up, or hand-cuffed. Perhaps, the most handsome of the women, she is composed and has always made a good impression. Like Muffet she knows the potential of being attractive. Unlike Muffet, she's not sure it's nice, or the right image to let people know. Katie always walks with direction and that's why it's fun to make her stop and laugh.

SAMANTHA STEWART: A gently attractive woman. If another old adage, "Smith is to bed and Holyoke is to wed" is true, it is women like Samantha who have secured Holyoke's side of the claim. Quiet, tasteful, yet one would always notice her at a party. However, she would be so gracious in finding out what you do, that her work would always remain a suspicion. Samantha is like a Shetland cable knit sweater, a classic. The daughter of the mayor of Naperville, she is closet wit, or she wouldn't have made the friends that she did in college.

RITA ALTABEL: In 1966 Rita Altabel won a D.A.R. scholarship to Mount Holyoke. In 1968 she walked through the Yale Cross Campus Library with the Yale Crew Team. Rita had cowbells on her dress. In 1976 she wasn't sure if the C.I.A. had put L.S.D. into all polyester shirts. But she knew it was only safe to wear cotton. Rita *refuses* to live *down* to expectations. She shouldn't worry about it. Her imagination would never let her.

AT THE COLLEGE

MRS. PLUMM: Housemother of North Stimson Hall. Mrs. Plumm, like the furniture is straight-backed but cozy. You can't help but giggle in her presence and grow fonder of her dignity with hindsight.

SUSIE FRIEND: Pink *Villager* sweater, Pink *Villager* skirt, pink knee socks, pink yarn in her hair, and *Weejuns*, of course. Susie Friend is head of freshmen, co-ordinator of Father-Daughter Weekend, Spring Weekend, Fall House Parties, the student-faculty committee on library responsibility, and never, unfortunately, gets exhausted.

CARTER: A frail girl in an oversized skirt and shirt that she wore all through prep-school. Carter may seem catatonic, but she has a rich inner life — though it is up to debate whether she is a genius or just quiet. She is inner-directed.

LEILAH: Leilah, like Kate is a handsome woman. In fact, she is second to Kate in her attractiveness and in her academic life. Leilah is serious and somehow seems distant from her friends. She is very tailored to the point of almost rigid. But behind her rigidity is a genuine kindliness and a strong intellect. Leilah's parents are probably high powered academics but she has not told them or her friends any of the fears and anxiety she is beginning to feel her senior year. Sometimes Leilah spends a great deal of time alone being admirable.

8

Uncommon Women
And Others

ACT ONE

SCENE 1

Handwritten annotation in right margin: "it's uncommon to be an individual woman to a real woman ? still need to retain their though femininity"

MAN'S VOICE. The college produces women who are persons in their own rights: Uncommon Women who as individuals have the personal dignity that comes with intelligence, competence, flexibility, maturity, and a sense of responsibility. This can happen without loss of gaiety, charm or femininity. Through its long history the college has graduated women who help to make this a better, happier world. Whether their primary contributions were in the home or the wider community, in advocations or vocations, their role has been constructive. The college makes its continuing contribution to society in the form of graduates whose intellectual quality is high, and whose responsibility to others is exceptional. (*As Man's Voice begins lights come up on Kate Quin making final adjustments on a restaurant table. Enter Samantha Stewart. They embrace. The Women speak softly to each other. As the Man's Voice fades, Kate gets up from the table and Holly Kaplan enters.*)

SAMANTHA. (*Laughs.*) Holly, it's nice to see you.

HOLLY. You too Samantha. You cut your hair.

SAMANTHA. Yeah, I didn't want to look like Jean Shrimpton anymore.

HOLLY. Katie. How long are you in town for?

KATE. I don't know. I'm here on a women and law conference. Very grown-up, huh? I am now the young spokesperson at all the obligatory boring occasions.

HOLLY. How's Robert?

SAMANTHA. Oh, he's fine. He was just cast in a T.V. pilot. He plays the male ingenue and he's worried 'cause his hairline is receding.

9

KATE. Holly, I forgot to tell you. Rita's coming down from Vermont. She told Samantha she had a six-year itch to see us all again.

SAMANTHA. Muffy wrote me and said that Rita was so fat at her wedding that she couldn't even walk down the aisle. She had to be lowered to the altar by a crane. (*Pause.*) I don't believe that.

MUFFET. (*Enters and joins the conversation immediately.*) Rita was a rotunda. It was pathetic when the orchestra played (*Begins to sing "More."*) "More than the greatest . . ." She must sit in bed and eat bon-bons all day.

KATE. Gross-me-out, Muffet.

ALL. Gross-me-out?

MUFFET. Holly, pumpkin. (*Kisses Holly and touches her hair.*) I like your hair. Kate, did you really have to bring your attache cast to the restaurant? Washington isn't that far away, I wish you got into town more often.

KATE. Muffet, I am a very important person now.

MUFFET. Don't you still sneak trashy novels?

HOLLY. I thought of you, Katie, when Jacqueline Suzanne died.

SAMANTHA. Did you know she had a buttocks enhancement? Eva La Gallienne told Robert when he was touring in *Cactus Flower.*

MUFFET. Samantha, only you would call an ass lift a "buttocks enhancement."

KATE. Who's Eva La Gallienne?

HOLLY. She wasn't our year. (*Pause.*)

MUFFET. Kate, how's Iki?

KATE. Well, he still loves me and Mother still asks about him. But . . .

MUFFET. And what's his name, the revolutionary. . . .

KATE. He left the bookstore and finished law school. He loves me, too. Muffet, this is adolescent. (*Pause.*) I've become a feminist.

HOLLY. Well, Alice Harwitch dropped out of medical school to form a lesbian rock band.

KATE. Gross-me-out! Does she sleep with women?

HOLLY. I guess so; they live together.

MUFFET. So what? I've taken a stand on birth control pills. I won't be manipulated by the pharmaceutical establishment.

HOLLY. Well, you're just not a masochist.

MUFFET. Oh, yes I am. I'm an insurance seminar hostess.

HOLLY. Muffy, why don't you go to graduate school?

10

MUFFET. Holly, not all of our fathers invented velveteen and can afford to send us to three graduate schools. Which master's are you on now; design, literature, or history. I can never keep track.

HOLLY. History.

MUFFET. Holly's embarrassed. You know I didn't mean it. You know you're my best. In fact, the one thing I miss in Hartford is having women friends. (*Pause.*) Did you read in the Alumnae Magazine that Nina Mandelbaum, now a landscape architect, got married twice to the same pediatric pulmonary specialist—they had a small wedding in Mexico and then a big religious ceremony in New York. Why Mexico? Do you think he went to medical school in . . .

ALL. Guadalajara!

HOLLY. My parents got a hold of that magazine and offered to fly me to Mexico if I thought he had any friends.

SAMANTHA. Did you know that Ca-Ca Phelps is teaching at Yale?

KATE. Stop!

HOLLY. She was one of those people who was with her horse the day of the Cambodia strike. Her real name was Caroline, right? So why does she still insist on calling herself Ca-Ca? Katie, wasn't Ca-Ca a friend of Leilah's?

KATE. I don't know. I really didn't know Leilah's friends very much. (*Quick pause.*) Do you ever think it's odd that none of us have children? I know we're the uncommon bell curve, but I still think it's odd. I can't decide if I want any.

MUFFET. Don't worry, Nina Manelbaum will bud for all of us. There's a good genetic pool in pediatric pulmonary specialists. (*Pause.*) So, where's Rita?

KATE. I don't understand what Rita's doing. She's a smart girl.

MUFFET. So what. We're all smart girls.

HOLLY. It's a sexist society.

KATE. I don't have any trouble.

MUFFET. Kate, you don't know what trouble is. You were born in *Holiday Magazine.*

KATE. Really, what does Rita do all day?

HOLLY. Nothing.

KATE. Gross-me-out! (*Rita enters. As Rita enters, she screams out each girl's name and kisses them. Finally, after going around, she kisses one girl twice.*)

RITA. I just called Timmy.

11

HOLLY. He loves you.

RITA. No, he waits on me. I told you I always wanted a wife. He gives great head though. (*Pause.*) Kate, I'm really getting into women's things. I've been reading Doris Lessing, and I think when I get it together I'm going to have a great novel.

MUFFET. Rita, how are you getting it together doing nothing?

RITA. I'm getting into my head.

MUFFET. (*To Holly.*) Or Timmy's as the case may be.

RITA. Kate, I want to hear more about your law firm. I think we need more women lawyers and gynecologists. I won't go to mine anymore, 'cause it's a man. Besides, I heard he had a twin.

SAMANTHA. Oh, but Rita, you really should get a regular check-up.

RITA. Samantha, what's it like being married to Robert?

SAMANTHA. We're very happy.

RITA. I had to train Timmy. He's going to become my Leonard Woolf. Got a match, Muffet?

SAMANTHA. I was going to join a woman's group, but I couldn't decide what to take—macrame, bread-baking, or consciousness rap. (*Muffet lights herself, Rita and Holly on one match.*)

RITA. You know I saw a Bette Davis movie once, and the third one on the match dies. (*Puts arm around Holly.*) I didn't upset you, Holly, sweetheart?

HOLLY. No, it was planned on my part. I hate the women's movement. I sent an article to *Ms.* and this Noel Schwartz, sent me back a personal note saying, "I was a heretic to the sisterhood." And I ask you, is Holly Kaplan that different from Noel Schwartz? And she telling me about the sisterhood!

MUFFET. She has problems.

RITA. That's all right, Holly, when we're forty, we'll be incredible.

HOLLY. Rita, when we were graduating, you predicted by thirty. (*Pause. Rita tosses it off.*)

RITA. At least at college they appreciated us.

HOLLY. No they didn't. You were miserable. You hated it.

RITA. Well, at least we appreciated us.

MUFFET. I wish I was back there.

KATE. That says something about the quality of your life. (*Pause.*)

HOLLY. Kate already is incredible.

KATE. I don't think I appreciated women then, as much as I do now.

12

RITA. Kate, you just lacked imagination.

KATE. Now, Carter, for example, was incredibly bright.

MUFFET. Now, Carter, for example, was a catatonic. (*Pause.*)

SAMANTHA. Wanna make an announcement?

KATE. What?

SAMANTHA. I'm going to make an announcement. Like at Mount Holyoke. Now, let's all pretend we're at the dining room table. (*All the girls clink their glasses.*) Seniors and anybody who will be here for graduation: We need people to sing on Upper Lake, Commencement Eve. Singers are needed both on shore and in canoes. We will be singing show tunes, and—special attraction—"Love Look Away," from *Flower Drum Song,* and of course, the Alma Mater. Questions call . . .

ALL. Susie Friend! (*All the girls clap and laugh. Holly standing up agitated and not laughing.*)

MUFFET. Holly, what's wrong?

HOLLY. I can't stand to hear clinking glasses. It always makes me feel at any moment someone will come out in one of those pastel *Modess* living rooms and tell me to take my feet off the table, dear. (*They all clink their glasses.*)

END SCENE

ACT ONE

SCENE 2

Mrs. Plumm enters as soon as the girls finish clinking. She addresses her speech to the audience. The speech will serve as a transition from present to past. The girls are seated behind her for the speech. It is possible she has prepared visual arm movements with her oral recitation, that the girls mimic from behind.

MRS. PLUMM. I'm so glad I have this opportunity to welcome all you girls to tea this year. I'm Mrs. Plumm, housemother of North Stimson Hall. Dear, take your feet off the table. The tea fund was established by Lucy Valerie Bingsbee, class of 1906, after whom a Vermont orchid bog was recently dedicated by Governor Hoff as The Lucy Valerie Bingsbee Wildflower Sanctuary. I think you girls will find tea here very comfy. I knew Lucy. I never cared for her much. I hope you all have a good year. There's a bit of a draft in here. If you have any questions or suggestions please knock at my door at any time except after 8:00 P.M. Although I'm not needed to sign overnight slips anymore, I'm still interested in all my girls. I thought before the end of tea, I'd read for you since I've always enjoyed oral interpretation. My friend, Dr. Ada Grudder, class of 1928 organized a theatre at the Christian Medical College in Nagpur, India. She begs me to visit, but I don't like long trips, and anyway it's so pleasant here, especially in the fall. Mmmmmmmmmmm. The cookies look lovely. What are they? Shortbread? I'd like to read from the poetry of Emily Dickinson class of 1850. To those of you who are familiar with this reading please bear with me. Contrary to rumor, I didn't know Emily. (*Laughs to herself*.) She never accepted visitors.

    The heart is the capital of the mind,
    The mind is a single state.
        heart and mind together make
    A single continent.

    One is the population
    Numerous enough.
    This ecstatic nation
    Seek—it is yourself.

(*She turns to girls at restaurant table*.) Please take your tea-cups to the long table at the end of the room when you leave. Why doesn't someone close the window? There's still a draft in here. (*Exit Mrs. Plumm*.)

END SCENE

ACT ONE

SCENE 3

A college living room. Six years earlier.

MAN'S VOICE. On November 8, 1837, Miss Lyons Seminary was a place of high excitement. The building had been completed for

14

the school that was to do for young women what Yale and Harvard were doing for young men. The 80 students who enrolled the first year had the vitality and dedication of pioneers. (*Same women as in first scene. They are joined by Leilah an attractive, but intense young woman. At one chair is also a very frail blond girl with alabaster skin, Carter. Also they are joined by Susie Friend, in tasteful* Villager *turquoise and engagement ring. The coffee table is set with tea-cups and milk and sugar, finger sandwiches and mayonnaise. The girls leave restaurant table and led by Susie Friend they stand up and perfunctorily sing grace. The attitude towards grace varies*)

ALL THE WOMEN. (*Sing.*)

Oh, the Lord is good to me,
and so I thank the Lord,
for giving me the things I need
the sun and the rain, and the appleseed,
the Lord is good to me.

(*Carter pulls out her chair. Susie Friend puts her hand on the chair.*)

SUSIE. Oh, no wait. You can't sit down 'til Mrs. Plumm comes.

CARTER. Who's Mrs. Plumm?

SUSIE. She's our housemother.

RITA. She has syphilis. (*Mrs. Plumm enters and sits behind a small tea service. Rita waves hello. The girls sit down in unison. Susie clinks her glass. All the girls follow in unison. Carter watches.*)

SUSIE. (*Stands up.*) Announcement, Announcement! There'll be sherry and dinner to honor senior choral members at 1886 House. Also congratulations to Melissa Weex and Ca-Ca Phelps, new chairman of the Outing Club and Swan Song Soiree . . . (*Everyone applauds. Rita and Kate applaud twice. Susie sits down. She takes a finger sandwich.*)

SAMANTHA. Susie, would you care for mayonnaise?

SUSIE. I couldn't.

MUFFET. Holly could.

SUSIE. (*Biting sandwich.*) I love finger sandwiches. I'm Susie Friend. (*Turns her head to Carter.*)

MRS. PLUMM. Tea's ready, girls. (*All the girls pick up their cups and form a line in front of Mrs. Plumm. First Susie, Kate, Rita Holly, then Samantha.*)

HOLLY. I'll get it for you, Muffy. (*Muffy and Carter are left on the couch. Mrs. Plumm pours first for Susie.*)

SUSIE. Thank you, Mrs. Plumm. Mrs. Plumm is my favorite house-mother. And Earl Grey. I love Earl Grey.

MRS. PLUMM. Dear, would you care for some brandy?

SUSIE. No, thank you. (*She turns to Kate.*) Kate, do you want a ride to Cambridge this weekend? (*Mrs. Plumm pours for Kate.*)

KATE. No, I'm staying here to work.

MRS. PLUMM. Care for some honey, dear? (*Leilah shakes her head. Kate and Susie walk back to the couch.*)

SUSIE. Well, if you ever need a ride to Cambridge, I go every weekend. (*They sit. Susie turns to Carter.*) I used to date Wharton, but that was before I knew what I wanted. (*Susie laughs at her own charm.*)

CARTER. Yes. (*Mrs. Plumm pours tea for Leilah. The girls take a slight notice of Carter.*)

MRS. PLUMM. Leilah, aren't you going to stay with us for tea?

LEILAH. No, I have more reading to do. (*Rita is in front of Mrs. Plumm.*)

RITA. I'd like brandy and honey.

SUSIE. (*To Carter.*) I'm a senior. Head of freshmen in North Stimpson Hall and a psychology major. (*Holly is in front of Mrs. Plumm.*)

MRS. PLUMM. Holly, dear I told you I can't permit you to come to tea in pants. It's not fair to the other girls. I'll let you stay this afternoon. But, dear, let's not see it happen again. I know you can do it, you looked very pretty at "Gracious Living" once. (*Samantha moves up to Mrs. Plumm and Holly. The girls at couch turn around to watch.*)

SAMANTHA. Holly is very pretty in pink.

HOLLY. I'm sorry, Mrs. Plumm.

MRS. PLUMM. Dear, I just don't want our house to get a reputation.

CARTER. Yes. (*All the girls are seated and served. Exit Mrs. Plumm. Girls look up at Carter.*)

MUFFET. You're not sorry. You loved every minute of it.

KATE. Holly, I don't see what difference it makes to you. Why torment her? It's just a waste of time.

HOLLY. I don't have a skirt.

MUFFET. Oh, come off it, Holly. Your father invented "velveteen."

RITA. I think Holly is very pataphysical.

SUSIE. You know, you girls should really sit at Mrs. Plumm's

16

table more often. I see your group running to the end table after she walks into the room.

CARTER. Yes. (*They look again.*)

SUSIE. Well, she's very sweet!

SAMANTHA. (*Sweetly to Carter.*) She doesn't really have syphilis.

SUSIE. Especially you, Kate. Mrs. Plumm admires you. And you could make some new friends. I notice your nice friend, Leilah never comes to dinner anymore. At least try sitting with Mrs. Plumm at "Gracious."

SAMANTHA. (*Smiles to Carter.*) Susie, she doesn't know what "Gracious Living" is.

SUSIE. Don't call a freshman "she." It's alienating. I learned that in psychology.

HOLLY. I think "Gracious" is a cultural excess. When I get out of here, I'm never going to have dinner by candlelight in the wilderness with 38 girls in hostess gowns. Unless, of couse, I train for Amazon guerrilla warfare at the Junior League. Also I can't stomach the way Mrs. Plumm's neck shakes when she pours the sherry. (*The girls all shake their necks.*)

SUSIE. Holly, have you ever been to "Gracious" at Smith? Ours is much more homey. I'm glad I didn't go there to college. Smith's much too social.

KATE. Not as much as Vassar. I applied there as a safety school.

SAMANTHA. Well, Vassar's just a cut above Connecticut College.

HOLLY. I thought Conn. was a good school.

MUFFET. If you like the Coast Guard.

KATE. Aren't Wellesley and Bryn Mawr the most academic?

SAMANTHA. Well, Bryn Mawr, of course. But Wellesley lacks imagination. They just marry Harvard and M.I.T.

HOLLY. Hands up! Who here got into Radcliffe? (*No hands go up.*)

MRS. PLUMM. (*Appearing briefly.*) Hands up! Who wants dessert? (*No hands go up.*)

KATE. Gross-me-out! It's last night's jelly rolls.

CARTER. Yes.

MUFFET. Don't be embarrassed, Holly. You can take them up to your room. (*Clinking glass noise is heard.*)

GIRL'S VOICE. (*Announces.*) Male Long Distance, Male L.D. for

Susie Friend. (*Susie throws her napkin on the table and runs out of the room singing, "Oh, the Lord is good to me."*)

RITA. Hi, I'm Susie Friend. I love finger sandwiches, Earl Grey, and Cambridge. I'm a psychology major, head of freshmen in North Stimson Hall, and I wax my legs. I'd let a Harvard man, especially from the Business or Law Schools violate my body for three hours; Princeton, for two hours and fifty minutes, because you have to take a bus and a train to get there; Yale, for two hours and forty-five minutes because my Dad went there and it makes me feel guilty; Dartmouth, for two hours and thirty minutes because it takes them time to warm up; Columbia, I just don't know, because of the radical politics and the neighborhood. I learned that in psychology. Now, if I could have a Wellesley girl, or Mrs. Plumm, that would be different.

KATE. Rita, you're so adolescent.

MUFFET. Remember when Rita made Rorschach tests with her menstrual blood to summon back Edvard Munch.

HOLLY. Rita, you couldn't go out with a nice boy from Amherst?

MUFFET. It was her interdepartmental project.

RITA. I thought it was very pataphysical.

CARTER. Yes.

SAMANTHA. But, Rita, you're still on the D.A.R. Scholarship.

KATE. Uch, Rita, gross-me-out!

RITA. I never let my economic background deter me.

SAMANTHA. Sometimes I wish I'd never left the Midwest.

MUFFET. Oh, Rita, you've upset her.

RITA. (*Arm around Samantha's chair.*) Samantha, pumpkin, why don't you make an announcement? (*Puts spoon in Samantha's hand and moves glass toward her.*) It'll make you feel better.

SAMANTHA. Rita, I've been here almost four years, and I've never made an announcement.

RITA. Well, it always makes Susie Friend feel better.

SAMANTHA. We don't belong to any committees.

HOLLY. Kate's in Phi Beta Kappa.

MUFFET. Holly, you do it. They'll never expect it from you. (*Holly, Kate, Samantha, Rita, Muffet clink their glasses. Holly stands up.*)

HOLLY. Um. Susie Friend has requested a toast. (*Holly, Kate, Samantha, Muffet immediately stand up and toast their tea-cups. Carter stares blankly.*)

18

HOLLY, KATE, SAMANTHA, RITA, MUFFET. (*All sing.*)*
    Tired of books and boring classes
    Drop your books, fill up your glasses
    Drink, the girls who think
    Of mixing Greek and Latin
    With a cool Manhattan
(*Susie Friend rushes back to the living room and toasts her tea-cup.
Mrs. Plumm enters, toasts and sings.*)
EVERYONE.
    And Amherst has its Heidelberg's
    And then there's Mory's down at Yale
    And when those Harvard boys
    Drink to College joys
    It's dull you must agree
    Adding lemon to your tea.

    Smith may have their Ice Tea Hours
    We prefer our whiskey sours.
    Drink and never think
    About tomorrow tonight.
(*They all clink each other's tea-cup. The girls take their napkins
and begin to exit.*)
SUSIE. There'll be a rule book test for all freshmen tonight in the
living room after "Gracious." Mrs. Plumm has promised to bring
sherry.
CARTER. Who's Sherry? (*Everyone does a double take look at
Carter. The girls begin to leave the living room. Each girl, as she
exits, folds her napkin and puts it into a box. Carter struggles
behind.*)
SAMANTHA. (*Watching Carter.*) Susie, she doesn't know where
to put her napkin.
SUSIE. Don't call a freshman "she." It's alienating. I learned that
in psychology. Hi, what's your name?
CARTER. Carter.
SUSIE. Well, Carter, we each have a separate napkin cubby com-
partment. We take them out and put them back after each meal.
Watch Kate fold her napkin. Your napkin, Carter, is washed and
pressed every Wednesday and Sunday in time for "Gracious."

* See note on copyright page concerning music for this song.

Now, your box is right to the left as you enter the dining room. *(Takes Carter's napkin, folds it, and puts it away in the napkin cubbyhole.)* And Carter if you have any questions or you just want to talk about psychology, knock on my door. It has the Snoopy calendar on it. I got the calendar as a present from Kenny at Harvard. I used to date Wharton but that was before I knew what I wanted. *(She winks at Carter.)* Good-night, oh, and Carter. I would avoid Rita. I don't know what the D.A.R. was thinking of. *(Blows her a kiss and exits. Carter is left sitting, looking at her napkin.)*

END SCENE

ACT ONE

SCENE 4

MAN'S VOICE. The real problem for many educated women is the difficulty they have in recognizing whether they have been a success. . . . Women will be part-time mothers, part-time workers, part-time cooks, and part-time intellectuals. When scholars point out that even the best cooks have been men, the proper answer is, "But what man has been not only the second best cook, but the third best parent, the seventh best typist, and the tenth best community leader?" Just like the pot of honey that kept renewing itself, an educated woman's capacity for giving is not exhausted but stimulated by demands. *(Muffet is reading the college catalog. Carter is silent and sits on the floor. Suddenly Muffet throws the book down.)*
MUFFET. I am so tired. Why doesn't someone just take me away from all.this? Did you ever notice how walking into Samantha's room is like walking into a clean sheet? She and Susie Friend celebrate Piglet's birthday. Katie says you're very bright. Did I tell you what happened in Chip Knowles' women's history class today? Do you know Chip Knowles? He always wears chamois shirts and Topsiders from L.L. Bean. You can never find anything you want in those L.L. Bean catalogues. So I just order a decoy duck every year. It makes me feel waspy. Chip's wife Libby, graduated first in her class from Vassar. When I told Chip I was a senior and didn't know what I'd be doing next year, Chip told me that Libby doesn't

20

really spend the day mopping and catching tadpoles with Chip, Jr. She may be mopping with her hands but with her mind she's reliving the water imagery in the Faerie Queen. Anyway, I thought women's history would be a gut and it wouldn't look as obvious on my record as "Marriage and the Family." As it turns out, this class isn't half bad. We read all the basics; the womb-penis inner and outer space nonsense. The Feminine Mystique, Sexual Politics, Mabel Dodge's Diary. Chip Knowles says women's history is relevant. Do you think women will lose their relevancy in five years? Like "Car 54, Where Are You?" Anyway, after two months of reading about suffragettes and courageous choices, this French dish comes into class dressed in a tight turtleneck and skirt. And you know how for seminar breaks everyone brings in graham crackers, well this chick brings in home made petit-fours. And she stands in front of the class and tells us she has not prepared her report on Rosie the Riveter because, "You girls are wasting your time. You should do more avec what you have down here— (*Muffet points to her breasts.*) then avec what you have up here." (*Muffet points to her head.*) And in less than five seconds the class is giving her a standing ovation, everyone is applauding. Except Holly and Rita, who grabbed the petit-fours, and ran out of the room in protest. I didn't do anything. I felt so confused. I mean this chick is an obvious imbecile. But I didn't think she was entirely wrong either. I guess the truth is men are very important to me. Well, not more important than you and Holly and Samantha. Well, not always, pumpkin. Sometimes I know who I am when I feel attractive. Other times it makes me feel very shallow like I'm not Rosie the Riveter. I suppose this isn't a very impressive sentiment, but I would really like to meet my prince. Even a few princes. And I wouldn't give up being a person. I'd still remember all the Art History dates. I just don't know why suddenly I'm supposed to know what I want to do. I guess I should think about sleeping with someone tonight to pass the time. Except it's always creepy in the morning. Rita doesn't think so. But she's promiscuous. I'm not promiscuous. I just hate going to bed alone. Maybe sometime you' can sleep on my floor. It's funny, you're a freshman and we're seniors. I'm not even worried about next year. I just have to make sure something happens to me. (*Enter Samantha. She is obviously excited.*)

SAMANTHA. Oh, hi Carter. (*Excited.*) Muffet, I'm in love.

MUFFET. With whom?

SAMANTHA. Robert Cabe. I met him last night and I thought this is the one I want. He's handsome and talented, and he's better than me and he'll love me. You'll see. I want to be his audience, and have my picture behind him, in my long tartan kilt in the *Times* Arts and Leisure Section.

MUFFET. That's nice Samantha. Samantha, how come I haven't met my Heathcliff yet?

SAMANTHA. Oh, Muffy, you wouldn't want him. They never settle down. Her soul wandered the moors for years. There's no security in that. You want someone who's good for you.

MUFFET. Maybe. (*Pause.*) Actually, I don't mind being alone. I like being strong. Like Rosie the Riveter.

SAMANTHA. I know, Muff. You're just more capable than me. Wanna go for a drive?

MUFFET. (*Begins to leave the room.*) Sure. (*Pause.*) Bye, bye, Carter.

SAMANTHA. Bye, Carter.

MUFFET. Oh, Carter, I should be back in about an hour or so, so why don't you come up then and we'll talk some more. (*Exit Muffet and Samantha.*)

END SCENE

ACT ONE

SCENE 5

Carter seated alone. Begins to ironically mime dance to the male voice. By the time she gets to "steadiness and gaiety," she sits down exhausted.

MAN'S VOICE. Although the attitude of society to education for women has changed in the last century and a quarter, the intellectual curiosity, hard work, and the spirit of adventure are still characteristic of Mount Holyoke. Mary Lyon, sending her early students out across the plains and seas as teachers and missionaries said, "Go where no one else will go. Do what no one else will

22

do." Some of her 25,000 "daughters" have blazed new trails, like Frances Perkins, Secretary of Labor under President Roosevelt. Others found adventure near at hand. Emily Dickinson went home. Today thousands of alumnae and students are serving their families and their communities with generosity and imagination, leading lives that enrich those they touch, ready to meet the unknown with steadiness and gaiety. (*Carter seated on the floor. Enter Susie Friend holding a note.*)

SUSIE. Hi, Carter. I have a message from your elf. You see, every freshman has a junior sister and a secret senior elf to help them through. That's right, it's your elf who's been leaving candy in your mail and napkin boxes and all the other treats, and she'll fix you up on the weekend and that's real neat. It's fun to see the girls at tea and Milk 'n Crackers too, and try and try to guess which one belongs to you. Don't you love Mrs. Plumm?? Fall teas are such fun when she brings apricot brandy. Mmmmmmmmmmmmm real yum! But Milk 'n Crackers is neat too. Every night the kitchen help leaves out crackers, milk, peanut butter, and sometimes fluff for you. You should come sometime, Carter. It's a real study break for me from my thesis on Claude Levi Strauss. I'm just a messenger here and I can't say who your elf is. But I think she's found you a male caller, hip horrah! See you later. (*Susie hands Carter the note and exits. Carter stares blankly at the envelope. She opens it, and Hershey kisses fall out. Carter reads the note.*)

CARTER.
    For our Carter
    No one's smarter
    Your elf has a surprise
    so open your eyes
    Kanga and Roo
    have a Yale blue for you.
(*She looks up.*)
    A terrific date
    He can't wait
    We'll double at the game
    but I won't be to blame
    if he's a little odd
    or a bit of a scrod
(*She looks back at Susie Friend.*)
    Hair by Thursday must be washed for the trip

It wouldn't hurt to give the split ends a snip
Tonite's the night it must be done
I'm sudsing with Ca-Ca and Jill in number one

Some Hershey kisses and best wishes
Bring a hot water bottle
See you at Milk 'n Crackers

Lovens,
Your elf
(*Carter puts down letter.*) Gross—me—out!

END SCENE

ACT ONE

SCENE 6

MAN'S VOICE. To profit most fully from the undergraduate curriculum, a student should examine for herself not only the nature of her academic interest, but also her conception of the good life and the kind of community she would like to fashion. (*Kate lies reading on a bed. She throws down the book she is reading and takes out another one.*)
KATE. (*Reading.*) "She remembered the way Melissa Blaine with her perfect cameo face had smiled up at Lance. 'Yes,' she said. 'I'm sure you've had most of the desirable women in the city, but I don't want to be among them.' Then, I think it's time I changed your mind, Lance said. Suddenly Lance's hand slid to the back of her gown. With one strong arm he pinned her to his chest so that try as she might, she could not push him away. He deftly unfastened the buttons of her gown, as if he had had long practice in performing such actions. "What are you doing? I'm not one of your strumpets!" (*Leilah knocks on the door. Like Kate she is very attractive. But as opposed to Kate, who is obviously quite confident, Leilah prefers to walk with her head down.*)
LEILAH. Kate? You're busy.
KATE. I was just reading "The Genealogy of Morals."

24

LEILAH. How was dinner?

KATE. Leilah, I don't understand why you never come. Even Susie Friend has been asking for you.

LEILAH. I came in to get the Nietzsche assignment.

KATE. Leilah, you don't think I'm a good person do you?

LEILAH. Kate, you're very good.

KATE. Then why don't you ever come in here just to visit instead of always asking for the assignment? Leilah, we roomed together for three years and now I never see you anymore. You're angry about last year in Greece. Aren't you?

LEILAH. That wasn't your fault.

KATE. I felt badly for you when both Iki and Thomas fell in love with me. Leilah, sometimes I think I should apologize to you and other times I don't know exactly what I should apologize for. I haven't done anything deliberately to hurt you. I want us to stay friends.

LEILAH. I know.

KATE. What are you going to do next year? I don't know what's going to happen if I don't get into Law School.

LEILAH. Kate, you're not supposed to hear until April; this is only November.

KATE. Well, I'm Phi Beta Kappa, but I'm worried about my Law Boards. (Pause.) Oh, Leah, pumpkin, don't worry. You'll be Phi Bet by June, in time for graduation. Just think you could be Muffet, or Samantha, or God forbid, Rita. What are they going to do with their lives? At least you and I aren't limited.

LEILAH. Did I tell you I applied to anthropology graduate school?

KATE. Why aren't you continuing in philosophy?

LEILAH. I really like anthropology. I want to go to small towns in Iraq. Look, I've made a list of Mesopotamia jokes.

KATE. Leilah, things aren't going to be better for you in Iraq. You don't have to make yourself exotic. You're a smart, pretty, girl. And anyway, if you can't leave your room in South Hadley, how are you going to get along in Iraq?

LEILAH. Just fine. Kate, what's the Nietzsche assignment? I have more reading to do.

KATE. You always have more reading to do. (Leilah begins to move away.) I'm sorry. Let's talk about something else. Like when we were roommates, okay? Leilah, what do you know about clitoral orgasms?

LEILAH. Well, my gentleman friend, Mr. Peterson, says they're better than others.

KATE. I wonder if I've had any.   *HA*

LEILAH. Kate, I'm sure you have. It's a fad.

KATE. Well, I never thought I had a problem.

LEILAH. Why don't you ask Rita?

KATE. Rita's fucked up. (*They laugh.*) Leilah, are you leaving philosophy because I'm Phi Bet and you're not? That's stupid. The department likes you as much as me.

LEILAH. Katie, I know you're trying but . . . I don't know. I just want to go away. I don't want to have to think about this place anymore. Kate, do you have the assignment?

KATE. Read the last two chapters in the "Genealogy of Morals." (*Pause.*) Look, Leilah, I'm sorry. I really am. But it's not my fault. You're always predisposed against me.

LEILAH. Kate, are you going to Milk and Crackers? I'll see you later.

KATE. Leilah, did you know Holly used to pick up men on the Yale green when she was a sophomore? She had clitoral orgasms. But that was a long time ago.

LEILAH. Maybe that's why she gets on with Rita. They have that in common.

KATE. Leilah, that's nasty.

LEILAH. (*Strongly.*) We all have hidden potential, Kate. (*Goes to exit.*) Bye Katie.

KATE. I'm going to ask Carter to join us for Milk and Crackers. I think she's very bright. It's been a long time since we've had someone new to talk to in this house, around three years. (*Frustrated, Kate goes back to her book.*) "I'm sorry," Lance said after a moment. "I suppose I shouldn't have done that. But you were asking for it. You wanted it. And you enjoyed every second of it."

END SCENE

ACT ONE

SCENE 7

Holly filling a diaphragm with orthocreme. Leilah and Rita are walking by, and as soon as they see Holly, they stop and watch.

26

there are men, there only fours, like a rooster

MAN'S VOICE. Am I saying that anatomy is destiny? No, it is not destiny. Providing a setting in which these subtle constraints may be overcome is particularly the mission of a college for women.

RITA. Holly, you've got enough orthocreme in there to sleep with the entire SS Constitution.

HOLLY. The instructions say two teaspoonfuls, so I thought I'd see what it's like with a little extra. I don't want to bud. (*Pause.*) Now that I have one of these things, whenever I see a boy with a yarmulke, I think he has a diaphragm on his head. (*Pause.*) I shouldn't have said that. I'll be struck down by a burning bush.

LEILAH. Who are you going to use this thing with?

HOLLY. I don't know. I got it 'cause it made me feel grown up. I could tell my friends stories about the day I got my diaphragm. Doesn't matter. In fact, I hate being mounted.

RITA. Holly, pumpkin, life doesn't really offer that many pleasures that you can go around avoiding the obvious ones.

HOLLY. What kind of pleasure? There's someone on top of you sweating and pushing and you're lying there pretending this is wonderful. That's not wonderful. That's masochistic.

RITA. But it can be your conquest, pumpkin.

LEILAH. This is distorted. Rita, you are manipulative.

RITA. Leilah, I'm not manipulative. Our entire being is programmed for male approval. Now, I, on the other hand, want abandonment. I want to do it with everything: dogs, cats, trees, bushes, ashtrays, children, light bulbs, shoe boxes . . .

LEILAH. Rita, don't you want some attachment? Some love?

RITA. From a cock?

LEILAH. Then why are you with Clark?

RITA. He's a wonderful lover. — *not typically masculine*

LEILAH. Clark's a homosexual.

RITA. He's creative. I've had enough of those macho types. Honestly, after I slept with Jack Hall he shook my hand and said thank you, and Chip Knowles came like a Pop Tart.

HOLLY. Really. Chip Knowles. I guess Libby was busy with the Faerie Queene.

LEILAH. But Rita, wouldn't you want the basis of a relationship to be some mutual understanding or . . .

RITA. (*Cuts her off.*) Leilah, you're beautiful. You can.

LEILAH. Rita, you're more beautiful than I am.

27

RITA. (*Rita demonstrates with her hand the vertical and horizontal qualities of the buildings and roads. At "shopping malls" she shows a parallel vertical with both hands.*) Listen, Leilah, this entire society is based on cocks— The New York *Times,* Walter Cronkite, all the building and roads, the cities, philosophy, government, history, religion, shopping malls, everything I can name is male. When I see things this way, it becomes obvious that it's very easy to feel alienated and alone for the simple reason that I've never been included because I came into the world without a penis. Therefore it is my duty to take advantage. Did I ever tell you about the time I left Johnny Cabot lying there after I'd had an orgasm and he hadn't. It was hilarious. And anyway, Leilah, no one will ever do for me what they'll do for you, or Kate, or even Samantha. So I have to take advantage. In my case it's a moral imperative. I've got to go now, I'm auditioning for Clark— He's directing a production of "Another Part of the Forest." (*She realizes Forest is another vertical.*) Forest, trees, logs, pinecones, elks . . . (*Exit Rita.*)

HOLLY. I think she's wrong about the shopping malls. (*Pause.*) Sometimes I think we have too much external and too little internal input. It's disturbing having sympathy with everyone's point of view. I guess I better put "thing" away in its shell.

LEILAH. Do you know the first time I ever really understood about diaphragms or sex was from reading *The Group.* I remember when I was twelve taking it down from my parents' library shelf and rereading the passages about Dottie leaving her diaphragm on Washington Square. It was quite titillating. And my parents didn't mind; they were happy I showed an early interest in Seven-Sister schools.

HOLLY. Lei, I want to tell you something but I was embarrassed to in front of Rita.

LEILAH. How can you be embarrassed in front of Rita, she's so embarrassing?

HOLLY. I called someone in Minneapolis today and hung up. I hung up twice.

LEILAH. Who was it?

HOLLY. A doctor I met with Muffet last summer. I thought I'd visit him over Christmas vacation. That's really why I bought "thing" here. He was very responsive on the phone. He said hello before I hung up.

LEILAH. Maybe you shouldn't see a friend of Muffet's.

28

HOLLY. Muffet doesn't know him either. We just met him once at a museum. I could tell he liked me. He smiled a lot at my legs. I'm very attractive from the kneecap to the ankle.

LEILAH. I guess I'm going to stay with my gentleman friend Mr. Peterson over vacation. Katie thinks he's boring.

HOLLY. He's not boring. See, I didn't want to talk to Minneapolis because I was afraid I'd start giggling and be self-effacing and my voice would screech. And then I'd start wishing I was Kate or Rita.

LEILAH. Holly, you can't keep wishing you're someone else. You'll be smothered.

HOLLY. Sometimes I want to clean up my desk and go out and say, respect me, I'm a respectable grownup, and other times I just want to jump into a paper bag and shake and bake myself to death.

SAMANTHA and SUSIE. (*Come through the room singing.*)

Happy birdle dirdle toodle yoodle doodle

Happy birdle dirdle toodle yoodle doodle

Happy birdle dirdle dear Piglet

Happy Birdle dirdle to you.

SUSIE. Make a wish.

SAMANTHA. Isn't he cute? (*They run out giggling. Leilah and Holly watch them. Leilah turns to Holly.*)

LEILAH. We could shake and bake Piglet.

END SCENE

ACT ONE

SCENE 8

Judy Collins record is heard.* Holly, Samantha, Kate. They are drinking sherry. It is very late.

SAMANTHA. (*Going to record player.*) This was my favorite song in high school. My senior year I sent it to a boy who was hitch-hiking cross country. I printed it on the back of a Vermeer

* See Special Note on copyright page.

29

postcard from the Chicago Art Institute. It was the only time I've ever written without capitals or punctuation. (*Pause.*) I also liked the Dave Clark Five a lot in ninth grade. I thought I could marry one of them cause they were more accessible than the Beatles.

KATE. My best was Leonard Cohen. When I was in high school, I wanted to go down like Suzanne with the garbage and the seaweed. Then I heard he had a thing with Joni Mitchell and there's only so much wistfulness one can stomach. (*Samantha continues to sing song. Enter Rita excited and triumphant.*)

RITA. I've tasted my menstrual blood.

KATE. Uch, Rita, gross-me-out.

RITA. Germaine Greer says the test of a truly liberated woman is tasting her menstrual blood.

KATE. Rita, that's drivel.

SAMANTHA. She also says women shouldn't wear underwear.

RITA. Who told you that?

SAMANTHA. Robert.

RITA. Robert. Robert, what does he know about it? I think all men should be forced to menstruate—Robert S. MacNamara, Baba Ram-Das, John Glenn—all of them except James Taylor, we'll spare him. But the rest of them should be forced to answer phones on a white naugahyde receptionist chair with a cotton lollipop stuck up their crotch.

SAMANTHA. Why spare James Taylor?

HOLLY. (*Looks at her surprised.*) Samantha!

SAMANTHA. Robert says I'm a closet wit. (*She giggles.*)

RITA. The only problem with menstruation for men is that some sensitive schmuck would write about it for *The Village Voice* and he would become the new expert on women's inner life. Dr. David Reuben, taking the time out to menstruate over the July Fourth Weekend, has concluded that "women are so much closer to the universe because they menstruate and therefore they seek out lemon freshened borax, hair spray and other womb related items." (*Pause.*) And that's why I think we need to talk about masturbation.

KATE. Rita, gross-me out!!

HOLLY. Rita, have you ever told the D.A.R. how you spend your time here?

KATE. (*Slightly interested.*) Do you really masturbate?

RITA. I know Susie Friend does. She does it in front of her

30

father's picture from *The New York Times* when he was made Vice President of American Canco.

SAMANTHA. (*Politely changing the subject.*) Anyone want some corn nuts? My mom just sent them from Naperville. You can't get corn nuts east of the Mississippi. (*Offers nuts.*)

KATE. I don't think Germaine Greer has thought this out properly. Know what I think the ideal society would be. If all women had communal apartments—not poured concrete socialist apartments—I mean an estate and everyone worked so child-care was rotated and the men came to visit on the weekends and were very nice and charming, bright—all those things—but they left on Mondays.

HOLLY. Katie, that's just what it's like here.

KATE. Well, except my plan doesn't get boring. The men who arrive are Arabian millionaires, poets, lumberjacks. Not corporate lawyers, or M.B.A's.

HOLLY. Katie, your're a snot rag.

RITA. Kate just grew up in *Holiday Magazine.*

SAMANTHA. I couldn't live in a society like that. I guess I'm not as strong as you, Kate.

RITA. Don't worry, Samantha, pumpkin. You're a closet wit.

HOLLY. I want to be divorced and living with two children on Central Park West.

KATE. Holly, don't you want to fall in love? You don't have to get married, but it would be nice to have a passion.

HOLLY. Yes, except if I fall in love it would be because I thought someone was better than me. And if I really thought someone was better than me, I'd give them everything and I'd hate them for my living through them.

KATE. You don't really expect to live through someone else, do you?

HOLLY. I think I'd like to very much.

KATE. Piffle, Holly. You're too diffuse. You need to concentrate your efforts.

RITA. Want to play a game?

KATE. Rita it's too late in the night for tampon bobbing.

RITA. This is a nice game for nice girls. (*Rita gathers the girls together. Pause.*) Let's each take a turn and say if we could marry any one of us who it would be.

SAMANTHA. I'm already pinned.

RITA. That doesn't count. You can only select from our own

uncommon pool. Holly, stop edging under the bed. (*Pause.*) I'd marry Samantha cause she'd make the best wife and in a matrimonial situation I could admire her the longest.

SAMANTHA. Would you really marry me?

RITA. Samantha, you're the perfect woman.

SAMANTHA. Rita, now I feel really badly cause I wouldn't have picked you and it would have been nice if everything worked out. (*Pause.*) This is very difficult 'cause it would be interesting to live with Rita, and Kate probably has the best future.

HOLLY. How 'bout Susie Friend?

SAMANTHA. You don't marry a girl like that. Too many committee meetings.. She'd never be home. (*Pause.*) Holly, you're sweet and funny but I couldn't support you and there would be a problem at the club. I guess I would marry Muffet cause she could get on with the outside world and Piglet wouldn't drive her crazy. Also, Muffet's glamorous, but she doesn't scare me.

HOLLY. I guess I would be most comfortable being married to Leilah or Rita. I'd never feel that I have to impress them. But when you get right down to it, I'd want to marry Katie. I would consider living through your accomplishments, Katie, and besides I'm sure if we got married my parents would approve and one of us would get our picture in the Sunday *Times.* (*They laugh.*)

SAMANTHA. How 'bout you, Kate? Who would you marry?

KATE. I don't know.

HOLLY. You don't have to marry me, Katie. I understand. Maybe you have to settle your career first.

KATE. I guess I never thought about marrying any of you.

RITA. Kate, for a smart woman you have a stunted imagination.

KATE. Well, if I married one of us I would probably have to be the main income source. That's excluding the possibility of trust funds. So if I was supporting someone I guess I would want to marry Carter.

HOLLY. Carter. Gross-me-out! (*Pause and giggles.*) I'm sorry. That wasn't very nice. I'm sure you'll be very happy together.

KATE. Carter is very bright. And if I'm going to be a boring lawyer then I'd want to be married to someone who would stay home and have an imagination. Anyway, Carter would *need* me. Holly, I would consider you cause you're such a good person. But then that would make me feel a little chilly.

RITA. I think we should celebrate.

SAMANTHA. What?

RITA. That none of our marriage proposals have been reciprocated.

SAMANTHA. We don't know. Maybe Muffy would want to marry me.

HOLLY. No. I think if we marry, we'll have to marry outside of each other. Probably men.

RITA. Muffy's out with pink pants. She knows she has to marry a man.

SAMANTHA. I know a great song we could celebrate with and dance to. (*She goes to record player and puts on a popular record celebrating love and marriage. The girls sing as soon as they hear it. They get up to begin dancing.*)

KATE. Do you think Germaine Greer remembers the night she danced with her best friends in a women's dormitory at Cambridge?

RITA. No, she was probably into dating and make-up. (*The girls are dancing and laughing.*)

HOLLY. Kate, you're a good dancer.

KATE. I know I should give up law and become a rock star.

SAMANTHA. Want to see the way Robert dances? (*She demonstrates. They laugh.*) It's pretty gross-me-out. (*Enter Carter who stares at them.*)

CARTER. I came in to tell you I've decided what I want.
I want to put Wittgenstein on film.

SAMANTHA. That's nice, Carter. Know what? (*She is giggling.*) We just all proposed to each other. And Kate said she'd want to marry you. Carter, Kate is really the best catch.

KATE. It was all hypothetical.

SAMANTHA. Carter, want to dance?

HOLLY. Don't you think Kate would make a great rock star?

KATE. Carter, dance with us. Just think how odd this would look if Susie Friend walked in. (*Carter begins to join them slowly. Her dancing is noticeably different from the other girls. A dying swan would be fitting. They continue to dance and laugh.*)

RITA. (*Over singing.*) Know what? I think when we're 25 we're going to be pretty fucking incredible. All right, I'll give us another five years for emotional and career development. When we're 30 we're going to be pretty fucking amazing. (*Pause.*) Carter, don't worry. You're younger so you have 13 years. (*They continue to dance and sing in a line. They move towards the back of the room. Holly goes to a phone in the corner. The girls dancing silhouette Holly from behind.)*

HOLLY. Operator, could you connect me with a Dr. Mark Silverstein in Minneapolis? (*She dials.*) Hello, is this Dr. Silverstein? Oh, this is his answering service. Hi! A message. (*Pause.*) Respect me. I'm a respectable grown up. Oh, my name is Simone de Beauvoir and I should be back in an hour. (*Holly hangs up and puts her feet up on the table as Mrs. Plumm enters. She is walking thru clinking a glass as if preparing to make an announcement. She stops at Holly.*)

MRS. PLUMM. Holly, dear, take your feet off the furniture. (*Exit Mrs. Plumm. Holly puts her foot back up and sits quietly while the music swells and girls continue to dance behind her.*)

END ACT ONE

ACT TWO

SCENE 1

Holly, Kate, Muffet, Samantha, Leilah, Susie, Rita, sing. Carter holds pitch pipe. The girls are standing for their performance.

ALL.
> Mildred, Maud and Mabel were sitting at their table.*
> Down at the Taft Hotel.
> Working on a plan to
> Catch themselves a man to
> Brighten up their lives a spell.

MUFFET. (*Whispers to her friends.*) I slept with a Whiffenpool at the Taft Hotel.

ALL. (*Sing.*)
> In their thirty years of proms,
> Never once had they had qualms,
> That they could fail to satisfy their craven
> Nor ever seemed to doubt it's not reckless to hold out
> For a son of Old New Haven.

RITA. (*Whispers.*) These women should have been in therapy.

KATE. (*Sings.*)
> And as they downed their pousse cafe

(*Whispers.*) I've been here four years and I still don't know what pousse cafe is.

ALL. (*Sing.*)
> The girls were heard to softly say.

SUSIE. (*Speaks.*) I want to welcome all you fathers to Father-Daughter weekend. You Dads look younger every year.

SAMANTHA. Hi, Daddy!

---

* See note on copyright page concerning music for this song.

35

RITA. Hi, Mr. Stewart. (*She winks. The girls work up some gestures for their performance during this part of the song.*)
ALL. (*Sing.*)

> Though we have had our chances
> With over night romances
> With the Harvard and the Dartmouth male.

> And though we've had a bunch in
> tow from Princeton Junction
> We're saving ourselves for Yale

RITA.

> Boola-Boola

ALL. (*Sing.*)

> For thirty years and then some
> We've been showing men some
> Tricks that make their motors fail

> And tho' we've all had squeezes
> From lots of Phdses
> We're saving ourselves for Yale

SUSIE. (*Sings.*)

> And when

ALL.

> Finally married we lie
> It will be with an Eli

SUSIE.

> Cause we're

ALL.

> Saving ourselves for Yale

CARTER. (*Raising her hand.*) I knew we had a purpose. (*The women curtsey for their fathers. Mrs. Plumm applauds and Susie Friend steps forward.*)

END SCENE

ACT TWO

SCENE 2

SUSIE. Hi! I'm Susie Friend, co-ordinator of Father-Daughter weekend, and I'm delighted to see so many of you Dads here.

36

First of all on behalf of the college, I would like to thank Holly Kaplan's father for his generous gift of 2000 slightly damaged velveteen bows. They're terrific. I'm sure they'll come in handy. Tomorrow night Mrs. Plumm has promised to play for us the white-breasted nuthatch tapes which she made last weekend on her annual spring birdwatch. And now our favorite housemother, Mrs. Plumm.

MRS.PLUMM. Welcome, fathers. This weekend has always been for me the highlight of the Spring Semester. My Junior year, my father stopped attending Father-Daughter weekend. You see that year, my birder classmate Ada Grudder and I had decided it was too dangerous for young girls to go on long bird watching trips unprotected. So I wrote home asking for money to buy a rifle. (*Pause.*) Gentlemen, please don't stop me if I go on too long. (*Pause.*) My father was appalled. He thought firearms did not provide an appropriate pastime for young women. And he feared I might be labeled eccentric. But I bought the rifle. Ada and I set up a firing range on Upper Lake where we re-enacted the Franco-Prussian War. For two years I received notes from home saying "Please marry Hoyt Plumm, and can't you teach bird watching at the High School." Finally, being a dutiful daughter, I did. Now if you will follow your daughters into the date parlour we can begin the dance. (*Girls begin to exit.*)

SAMANTHA. This way, Daddy. (*Rita winks again.*)

MRS. PLUMM. Could you put out that cigar, dear?

END SCENE

ACT TWO

SCENE 3

MAN'S VOICE. In the growth of tradition from the time of its founding by Mary Lyon to the present day the College continues to believe that the acquisition of knowledge of itself is not enough. Indeed, employers of graduates of the college seem to be looking for a readiness to work hard at learning unfamiliar techniques.

LEILAH. (*Muffet is putting on make-up. Leilah enters carrying a chocolate bunny.*) Muffy, this package just came for you.
MUFFET. What is this? "For my Muffet. I can't bluff it. An Easter Bunny for my pixie honey."
LEILAH. Is that from Susie Friend?
MUFFET. Christ no! It's from her father. Look, it's signed—Lovens, E. Courtland "Kippy" Friend. He was behind me in the bunny hop at the Father-Daughter weekend. Leilah, do you think I should plan to marry Kippy Friend? It's two months before graduation and I still don't know what I'm going to do next year. But I am prepared for life. I can fold my napkin with the best of them. Leilah, do you want this? I'll give it to Holly, she'll eat it.
LEILAH. I asked my father not to come up this year. Actually, my freshman year he came to Father-Daughter weekend and kept dancing with Katie and telling me how lucky I was to have such a good friend. Kate told him I was the prettiest and the brightest girl here. Ever since then, I make it a point to be busy doing research every Father-Daughter weekend. (*Throws down books.*) Oh, I can't wait to get out of here. I've booked a flight to Iraq for the day after graduation.
MUFFET. Really, Leilah, that's odd. You're very odd.
LEILAH. I won a fellowship.
MUFFET. Pink Pants is leaving right after graduation also. Lei, if he calls would you tell him I went away for the weekend? We had another fight yesterday.
LEILAH. What happened?
MUFFET. Nothing. He told me that next year he wants to work his way around the world on a freighter. I tried to appear like "sure," "that's fine," "Have a nice trip," "send a postcard." I don't understand why when Samantha meets someone suddenly she's pinned and when I want someone they tell me I'm being clutchy and putting too much pressure on them. I don't want any commitment. I like being alone.
LEILAH. Me too.
MUFFET. Leilah, where do women meet men after college? Does Merrill Lynch have mixers with Time Life staffers at the General Foods Media department?
LEILAH. I don't know who I'll meet in Iraq. I like that. Katie says I'm escaping. I think I just need to be in a less competitive culture.

38

MUFFET. Why does Katie bother you so much?

LEILAH. Excuse me?

MUFFET. I can't understand why Katie bothers you so much.

LEILAH. She doesn't. I like Katie. She's exceptional.

MUFFET. Katie has no hips.

LEILAH. It could be Social Darwinism. Katie could simply be a superior creature.

MUFFET. Pink Pants says you're prettier than Katie.

LEILAH. Sometimes when I'm in the library studying, I look up and I count the Katies and the Leilahs. They're always together. And they seem a very similar species. But if you observe a while longer the Katies seem kind of magical, and the Leilahs are highly competent. And they're usually such good friends—really the best. But I find myself secretly hoping that when we leave here Katie and I will just naturally stop speaking. There's something . . . (*Leilah begins to cry.*) It's not Katie's fault! Sometimes I wonder if it's normal for a twenty-year-old woman to be so constantly aware of another woman . . . "Thoughts of a dry brain in a dry season."

MUFFET. (*Suddenly concerned for Leilah.*) Mrs. Plumm thinks about Ada Grudder often.

LEILAH. If we did stop speaking she wouldn't even notice, or if she did, she'd just think she wasn't a good person for a day. I just want to get out of here so I'm not with people who know me in terms of her.

MUFFET. Leilah, why don't you come out with me tonight? I've always wanted to do this. We can go to a bar, not sleazy but also not a place where two nice girls usually go. And we'll sit alone, just you and I, with our two Brandy Alexanders and we won't need any outside attention. We'll be two uncommon women, mysterious but proud. (*Muffet puts her arm around Leilah.*)

LEILAH. All-right. I'd like that.

MUFFET. (*Honestly.*) Leilah, I do understand a little. It's debilitating constantly seeing your worth in terms of someone else.

VOICE. Male L.D. for Muffet DiNicola. Muffet DiNicola, Male L.D.

LEILAH. I'll take it for you Muffy.

MUFFET. (*Pauses and then gets her coat.*) No, it's got to be Old Pink Pants. Would you sign an overnight slip for me? See, Leilah, I know myself and as soon as the phone rings, I'm just fine.

(Muffet leaves with her coat. Leilah is left alone in the room holding the chocolate bunny.)

END SCENE

ACT TWO

SCENE 4

MAN'S VOICE. A liberal education opens out in many different directions; when intellectual experience is a real adventure, it leads toward the unfamiliar. Students at the college are expected to encounter a wide range of opportunities— That is to say uncertainties. A maturing mind must have an ethical base, a set of values, and wonder at the unknown.

(Rita, Holly, Kate, Muffet, Carter and Susie Friend, and Leilah, are in the living room. There is a large jar of peanut butter and fluff and some crackers on the table. They are putting large globs of fluff on their fingers and crackers.)

RITA. I think if I make it to thirty I'm going to be pretty fucking amazing.

HOLLY. My mother called me today and told me she saw a 280 pound woman on Merv Griffin, who had her lips wired together and lives on *Fresca*. She offered me a lip job as a graduation present.

MUFFET. Pass the fluff.

KATE. This stuff is vile. I bet the kitchen help took home the desserts. *(Samantha runs excitedly into the room.)*

SAMANTHA. I have something to tell you. I'm getting married to Robert. *(She starts to sing to the melody of Offenbach's "Can-Can.")*

> I'm leaving here
> Goodbye to all of you
> Things are just beginning
> And I can't stop grinning.
> *(She starts doing kicks and humming the song.)*
> Da-da-da-da-da-da-da
> Da-da-da-da-da-da-da
> *(She goes into the finale.)*

Things are beginning and
I'm grinning through my tears
Goodbye my friends
I'll miss you all through the years
The date is set for June
Da-dum-da-dum-da-dum
Da-da!

(*Nobody moves. The women throughout the song have been frozen.*)

SUSIE. Samantha, NO.

SAMANTHA. Yes.

SUSIE. NO.

SAMANTHA. YES.

SUSIE. NO.

SAMANTHA. YES.

SUSIE. Let's run and tell Mrs. Plumm. (*Susie and Samantha exit squealing no, yes . . . There is silence for a few moments. Carter continues to eat.*)

MUFFET. How come Carter eats so much Milk n' Crackers every night and never gains weight?

CARTER. I throw up immediately afterwards.

END SCENE

ACT TWO

SCENE 5

MAN'S VOICE. The college fosters the ability to accept and even welcome the necessity of strenuous and sustained effort in any area of endeavor. (*Enter Rita in denim jacket and cap.*)

RITA. Hey, man wanna go out and cruise for pussy?

SAMANTHA. Beg your pardon?

RITA. Come on, man.

SAMANTHA. (*Putting hair brush in her mouth as if it were a pipe.*) Can't we talk about soccer? Did you see Dartmouth take us? They had us in the hole.

RITA. I'd sure like to get into a hole.

SAMANTHA. Man, be polite.

RITA. (*Gives Samantha a light punch on the arm.*) Fuck, man.
SAMANTHA. (*Softly at first.*) Shit man. (*She laughs hysterically.*)
RITA. Fucking "A" man.
SAMANTHA. Excuse me.
RITA. Samantha, you're losing the gist.
SAMANTHA. I just feel more comfortable being the corporate type. Won't you sit down? Can I get you a drink? Want to go out and buy *Lacoste* shirts and the State of Maine?
RITA. (*Picking up Samantha's bag of nuts.*) Nice nuts you got there.
SAMANTHA. Thank you. You can only get them west of the Mississippi.
RITA. (*Chewing on the nuts.*) I'll give you a vasectomy if you give me one. (*Pause.*)
SAMANTHA. (*She breaks her male character.*) Rita, I liked the game when we said who we would marry much better. All right. (*She goes back into character.*) Anyway, I don't want a vasectomy. I like homes and babies.
RITA. (*Rita picks up Piglet.*) Hey, man what's this? You got a fucking doll, man, with two button eyes, a pink little ass, and a striped T-shirt. I could really get into this. This dollie got a name, man? Piglet?
SAMANTHA. (*Disliking game.*) I don't know.
RITA. What's the matter, man? You afraid I think you're a pansy or something?
SAMANTHA. (*Drops character.*) Rita, cut it out.
RITA. Samantha, I'm only playing.
SAMANTHA. We're twenty-one years old and I don't want to play.
RITA. Then why do you have the fucking doll?
SAMANTHA. (*Taking doll, she begins to exit.*) I like my doll. I've had it ever since my Dad won it when I was in sixth grade at the Naperville Fair.
RITA. (*Dropping doll and character.*) Samantha, you don't like me.
SAMANTHA. I like you, Rita. We're just very different. And I don't want to play anymore.
RITA. Do you know what, Samantha? If I could be any one of·us, first I would be me. That's me without any embarrassment or

neurosis—and since that's practically impossible, my second choice is, I'd like to be you.

SAMANTHA. But, Rita, when you're thirty you'll be incredible.

RITA. Samantha, at least you made a choice. You decided to marry Robert. None of the rest of us has made any decisions.

SAMANTHA. (Pause.) Thanks, Rita.

RITA. Well, I don't want to spend oodles of time with you. You're not a fascinating person. But I do want to be you. Very much. (Pause.) You're the ideal woman.

SAMANTHA. Robert says that I never grew up into a woman. That I'm sort of a child woman. I've been reading a lot of books recently about women who are wives of artists and actors and how they believe their husbands are geniuses, and they are just a little talented. Well, that's what I am. Just a little talented at a lot of things. That's why I want to be with Robert and all of you. I want to be with someone who makes a public statement. And, anyway, if I'm going to devote my uncommon talents to relationships, then I might as well nurture those that are a bit difficult. It makes me feel a little special.

RITA. (Taking Samantha's hand.) You are special, Samantha. We're all special.

SAMANTHA. It's a quiet intelligence. But I like it. (Pause.) Hey, Rita when's your birthday? Because when we get out of here, we probably won't see each other very much. But I want to be sure to send you a birthday card. I like you, Rita.

RITA. It's March 28. I'm an Aries. Aries women are impulsive and daring, but have terrible domineering blocks.

SAMANTHA.
    March 28 is the day of Rita's birthday, hipooray.
    She talks of cocks and Aries blocks
    But what's so neeta, about my Rita
    Is I know secretly, she's very sweeta.
(Starts to giggle.) Pretty fucking gross, man, huh! (She gives Rita a light punch and they begin to exit together.)

RITA. (Gives her a light punch and starts to giggle.) Yeah, pretty fucking gross, man. (Scene ends as they continue to giggle and exit with their arms around each other.)

END SCENE

43

ACT TWO

SCENE 6

MAN'S VOICE. The college maintains that along with knowledge, compassionate understanding is a central human activity. (*Carter is sitting on the floor typing rhythmically to the Hallelujah Chorus. Enter Kate who turns off the music.*)

KATE. Carter, do you think I'm boring? I was just reading Wittgenstein and I tried to imagine the film version. I even lit a candle and tried to imagine the film version and all I could come up with is you're very weird. See Carter, you can interrupt me if you want, I've always thought it's a waste of time to scatter one's energy. I'm not saying you're wasting your time making Wittgenstein films. They're certainly not redundant, and it's a good field for women, but the possibility would never occur to me. Carter, I'm afraid that I'm so directed that I'll grow up to be a cold efficient lady in a grey business suit. Suddenly, there I'll be, an Uncommon Woman ready to meet the future with steadiness, gaiety and a profession, and what's more I'll organize it all with time to blow dry my hair every morning. Tonight everything seems so programmed. Just once it would be nice to wake up with nothing to prove. Sometimes I wonder what I'd do if I didn't work or go to school for a while. But if I didn't fulfill obligations or be exemplary, then I really don't know what I'd do. I have a stake in all those uncommon women expectations. I know how to do them well. I don't mind that you're not chatty. Neither am I. Do you know that I've slept with more men than Muffet or Rita. Really, it's true, I like sex with irresponsible people. It's exciting, like a trashy novel. But I couldn't live with anyone irresponsible. Gross-me-out. Carter, I admire you. I really do. Sometimes I think you'll let me into your world which is more interesting, well, more imaginative than mine. When I'm around Holly and Muffet I congratulate myself on being such a well prepared grown-up. But I'm always watching myself. When I'm with you I'm not watching myself. I feel comfortable. Isn't that odd, Carter. You're not specifically a comforting person. Maybe we have that in common. I feel as if I'm under-articulating. (*Pause.*) I came in here cause I just got into Law School and I don't think I should go. I don't want my life to simply fall into place. (*Pause.*) Carter, can I sit here for a

44

while? I'm frightened. (*Carter begins to put her arm around Kate. Kate pulls back.*) No, that's all right, pumpkin. I'll just sit here for a while and then go back to work. (*Carter goes back to her typing. Kate, getting up.*) Why have you typed, "Now is the time for all good" twenty-five times?

CARTER. I am cramming for my typing test. I need fifty words per minute to get a good job when I get out of here. (*Kate puts the Hallelujah Chorus back on. Music swells as Carter continues to type.*)

END SCENE

ACT TWO

SCENE 7

MAN'S VOICE. The college places at its center the content of human learning and the spirit of systematic disinterested inquiry. (*It is late. The women are all studying. Kate looks up from her book.*)

KATE. Holly, did you ever have penis envy? *freud*

HOLLY. I beg your pardon?

KATE. Did you ever have penis envy?

HOLLY. I remember having tonsilitis.

KATE. Have you, Samantha?

SAMANTHA. I know I never had it. Robert's was the first one I ever saw. I didn't even know men had pubic hair.

KATE. How big was Robert's? Holly, don't fall asleep. This may be the last chance we have to accumulate comparative data. We're graduating in two more weeks. Now I remember Thomas' was around this big. That's small to medium with a tendency towards tumescence, and Iki was around this big. But it was curved so you can't trust my estimation. In fact, if I can remember the others were all kind of average. Oh, yeah, except for Blaise. His really did stand out. It was the biggest I ever saw. Except it was just like him. Large, functional, and Waspy. (*Kate may demonstrate size with a pencil and break it in half to show a smaller variety.*)

HOLLY. I knew a boy at Columbia with three balls. Really. He

45

came up to see me my freshman year because his psychiatrist said I wouldn't mind.

KATE. Did you sleep with him?

HOLLY. I didn't want to hurt his feelings.

KATE. Holly, you're such a mealy-mouth.

HOLLY. I didn't care. I guess I don't like men's underwear. Especially when they don't remove it and it's left dangling around one ankle. In fact, if you'd like a run down of every flacid appendage in the Ivy League, I can give you details.

KATE. I've never been with an impotent man.

HOLLY. You haven't lived.

KATE. Listen to this! This is from a chapter in Chip Knowles' new book· *Women My Issue.* Chip has concluded, and I quote. "That the discovery at four months that a girl is castrated is the turning point in her road. At fourteen months little girls fingers and pacifiers are introduced into the vagina and at fifteen months a girl baby has been known to fall asleep with her genitalia on her Teddy bear. Finally, at sixteen months they start using a pencil."

SAMANTHA. Don't little boys use pencils?

HOLLY. No, they write with their cocks.

SAMANTHA. But don't men have breast and womb envy?

KATE. Well, if they have it, they just become creative or cook dinner every now and then.

HOLLY. I guess I envy men. I envy their confidence. I envy their options. But I never wanted a fleshy appendage. Especially a little boy's. Whenever I get fat I get nauseated because it looks like I have one in my pants. (*Pause.*) Katie, this is nonsense. The only people who have penis envy are other men.

KATE. You mean it's all those appendages compensating for being small?

HOLLY. Yeah.

SAMANTHA. Well, I know I wouldn't want one 'cause then I couldn't have Robert's. What time is it?

KATE. 2 a.m.

SAMANTHA. I gotta go to bed, I have an Art History final in the morning.

KATE. Good night, pumpkin. (*Pause.*) Holly, do you think I have penis envy?

HOLLY. Oh, Katie, gross me out!

KATIE. No, really for me it's entirely possible.

HOLLY. You don't have it. (*Enter Rita frazzled. She immediately throws herself on a bed or couch.*)

RITA. You don't have what?

KATE. Nothing. Rita, what's the matter?

RITA. (*She goes into a womb position.*) I can't sleep.

HOLLY. What's wrong Rita?

RITA. (*Gets up.*) Nothing. I keep having recurrent *Let's Make a Deal* dreams . . . and my future is always behind the curtain, and the audience is screaming at me, NO, NO TAKE THE BOX! TAKE THE BOX! I haven't told anyone, but yesterday I went to New York, on a job interview. It was for one of those, "I graduated from a seven sister school and now I'm in publishing jobs."

KATE. Did you get the job?

RITA. I did very well at the interview. I told the interviewer that I was an English Composition Major, and I liked Virginia Woolf and Thackeray, but I really want to assistant edit beauty hints. I told her yes I thought it was so important for women to work and I would continue to write beauty hints even with a husband and family. The big thing at these interviews is to throw around your new found female pride as if it were an untapped natural resource.

HOLLY. Did you get the job?

RITA. Holly, don't be so result oriented. Anyway, at the end of the interview she told me it was delightful, I told her it was delightful, we were both delightful. She walked me to the door, and said, "Tell me dear, do you have experience with a Xerox machine?" I said, "Yes. And I've tasted my menstrual blood."

KATE. Rita, you didn't really do that, did you?

RITA. I did. Holly, I can't go to one of those places. I don't know what I'm going to do, but it's not going to be that. I'm not going to throw my imagination away. I *refuse* to live down to expectation. If I can just hold out 'til I'm thirty, I'll be incredible.

HOLLY. Rita, I think you're already incredible.

RITA. Actually I do have a new fantasy that helps me deal with the future. I pretend that I am Picara in a picaresque novel and this is only one episode in a satiric life. (*Rita gets up.*) Hey pumpkins, let's go down and hit the candy machine and see how much weight we can gain in a night.

KATE. All right, I should do one kinky thing before we graduate.

HOLLY. No, I have more work to do.

47

RITA. (*Triumphant again.*) And when the candy machine is empty, I'm going to start writing my novel. (*Kate and Rita exit.*)

HOLLY. (*Alone. She puts on the tape player and lies down on the bed smoking. A recording of James Taylor.* She reaches to the telephone and dials, and puts her raccoon coat over her for comfort.*) Operator, I'd like the phone number of a Dr. Mark Silverstein in Minneapolis, Minn. Could you connect me with that number please? Thank you. Hello, can I speak to Mark? Oh, do you have his number in Philadelphia? Thank you. No, that's all right. I'll call him there. (*Dials again.*) Hello, may I please speak to Mark? Oh, Hi. My name is Holly Kaplan. I met you last summer at a museum with my friend Muffet. It was the Fogg Museum. Oh that's all right, I never remember who I meet at museums either. (*She giggles.*) What's new? I'm not quite certain what I'll be doing next year. I'm having trouble remembering what I want. My friend Katie says I'm too diffuse. You'd like Katie. She's basing her life on Katherine Hepburn in *Adam's Rib.* She didn't tell me that but it's a good illustration. No, I haven't been back to the Fogg Museum this year. My brother goes to Harvard Medical, Business, and Law School. Maybe I'll move to Philadelphia. (*She giggles.*) I'm in North Stimson Hall, fourth floor, under my raccoon coat. I guess everything's all right here. I just like being under my coat. Last week when I was riding the bus back from Yale and covering myself with it I thought I had finally made it into a Salinger story. Only, I hated the bus, college, my boyfriend and my parents. The only thing really nice was the coat. (*Pause.*) I take that back about my parents. Do you know what the expression "Good Ga Davened" means? It means someone who davened or prayed right. Girls who good ga davened did well. They marry doctors. and go to Bermuda for Memorial day weekends. These girls are also doctors, but they only work part-time because of their three musically inclined children, and weekly brownstone restorations. I think Mount Holyoke mothers have access to a "did well" list published annually, in New York, Winnetka, and Beverly Hills, and distributed on High Holy Days and Episcopal bake sales. I'm afraid I'm on the waiting list. (*Pause.*) You were on the waiting list for Johns Hopkins. I have a good memory for indecision. My mother says doctors take advantage unless you're thin. And then they want to marry you and place you among the good ga davened. She says girls who have their own apartments hang towels from the windows so the men on the street know when to come up. My friend Alice Harwitch is becoming a doctor and I've never seen her enter a strange building with towels in the windows. Of course, she's a radical lesbian. Sorry to have bothered you. Hey, maybe you'd like to visit here sometime, it's very pretty in the spring. We could see Emily Dickinson's house and buy doughnuts. I think about her a lot. And doughnuts, I think about them a lot too. No, I don't write poetry, and I haven't read *The Bell Jar*. My friend Rita has. I don't know who Rita's basing her life on. Sometimes I think she'd like to be Katherine Hepburn, but Katie has the Katherine Hepburn market cornered and we're all allowed only one dominent characteristic. I'm holding a lottery for mine. *(She giggles again.)* Yes, I guess I do giggle a lot, and I am too cynical. I had my sarcastic summer when I was sixteen and somehow it exponentially progressed. Leilah, she's my nice friend who's merging with Margaret Mead, says sarcasm is a defense. Well, I couldn't very well call you up and tell you to move me to Minneapolis and let's have babies, could I? *(Her tone of voice changes.)* Well, sorry to have bothered you. Really, I'm fine. I find great comfort in Lay Lady Lay, One Bad Apple Don't Spoil The Whole Bunch Girl, and my raccoon coat. And I like my friends, I like them a lot. They're really exceptional. Uncommon women and all that drivel. Of course, they're not risky. I'm not frightened I'll ruin my relationship with them. Sometimes I think I'm happiest walking with my best. Katie always says she's my best, shredding leaves and bubble gum along the way and talking. Often I think I want a date or a relationship to be over so I can talk about it to Kate or Rita. I guess women are just not as scary as men and therefore they don't count as much. *(Holly begins to cry.)* I didn't mean that, I guess they just always make me feel worthwhile. *(Pause.)* Thank you, I'm sure you're worthwhile too. *(She is resigned.)* If it's all right, I'm not going to tell Muffet I called you. Muffet's the girl who was with me in the museum. Oh, that's all right. Well, thanks for talking to me. Goodbye, thank you. I guess so. *(Holly gets down on the bed. Turns the tape player back on. Slides the raccoon coat over her head. Music swells. Lights fade out.)*

END SCENE

ACT TWO

Scene 8

Pomp and Circumstance music is heard under the male voice. The girls march in and form a line behind Mrs. Plumm's tea service.

MAN'S VOICE. Commencement brings a whole set of new opportunities, as varied as they are numerous. By the time a class has been out ten years, more than nine-tenths of its members are married and many of them devote a number of years exclusively to bringing up a family. But immediately after commencement nearly all Mount Holyoke graduates find jobs or continue studying. Today all fields are open to women, and more than fifty percent continue in professional or graduate school. Anyone of a variety of majors may lead to a position as Girl Friday for an Eastern Senator, service volunteer in Venezuela, or assistant sales director of *Reader's Digest.* (*Lights up on Mrs. Plumm seated in the living room. Kate walks up to Mrs. Plumm.*)

MRS. PLUMM. What are your plans, dear?

KATE. I'm starting Harvard Law School in the fall.

MRS. PLUMM. Good luck, dear. (*Mrs. Plumm hands Kate a tea-cup. Kate sits. Leilah moves up to Mrs. Plumm.*) What are your plans, dear?

LEILAH. I'm studying anthropology in Mesopotamia.

MRS. PLUMM. Good luck, dear. What are your plans, Susie?

SUSIE. I'm becoming a security analyst, for Morgan Guarantee Trust.

MRS. PLUMM. Good luck, dear. (*Susie kisses Mrs. Plumm.*) What are your plans, dear?

SAMANTHA. As you know, I'm marrying Robert Cabe. He's going to be a successful actor.

MRS. PLUMM. Good luck, dear. (*The good luck, dear here is said in a different tone than it was to Kate. Mrs. Plumm hands Samantha a tea-cup. Samantha sits. Holly moves up to Mrs. Plumm.*) Holly, dear. Have you thought about Katie Gibbs? It's an excellent business school. (*Mrs. Plumm hands Holly a cup. Holly leaves the cup and sits. Enter Muffet.*) What are your plans, dear?

MUFFET. I'm assuming something is going to happen to me. I

50

figure I have two months left. (*Muffet giggles and Mrs. Plumm giggles.*)

MRS. PLUMM. Good luck, dear. (*Rita moves up as Muffet sits down and she immediately starts talking.*)

RITA. Well, God knows there is no security in marriage. You give up your anatomy, economic self-support, spontaneous creativity, and a helluva lot of energy trying to convert a male (half person) into a whole person who will eventually stop draining you, so you can do your own work. And the alternative—hopping onto the corporate or professional ladder is just as self-destructive. If you spend your life proving yourself, then you just become a man, which is where the whole problem began and continues. All I want is a room of my own so I can get into my writing. I was going to marry Clark, but he advertised himself as a houseboy in *The Village Voice* and I didn't want damaged goods. . . .

MRS. PLUMM. (*Cutting Rita off.*) I'm afraid our time is up, dear. (*Rita grabs a cup to toast Mrs. Plumm, and sits down. Mrs. Plumm gets up to address the audience, with the graduates sitting beside her.*) You are all to be congratulated on your graduation. And thank you. I certainly didn't expect such an elaborate party for my retirement. I'm so glad to see so many students, faculty, and friends—Dr. Ada Grudder, who travelled here all the way from Nagpur, India. Many memories, seasons, and teas come to mind. But I thought I'd share with you some recent thoughts. At my last Milk 'n Crackers at the college I had an interesting talk with Kate Quin, an articulate young woman, who told me somewhat wistfully that she thought my retirement and the recent student vote to abolish "Gracious Living," marked the end of an era. I have seen the world confronting Kate and her classmates expand—The realm of choices can be overwhelming. However, those of you who have known me as the constant dutiful daughter of my Alma Mater, and my family, may be surprised to know that I do not fear the change for my girls, nor myself. My work here completed, I plan to go on a little adventure. Next summer I will travel to Bolivia which is the heartland of ornithological variety on this planet. My dear friend Ada, has returned to me our trusty rifle. So you see, girls, perhaps even I am in a transition period. (*When Mrs. Plumm mentions Ada Grudder the girls look out to the audience for her.*) Am I cavalier about leaving gracious-living and tea? Hardly. You see as a housemother and teacher most often I have found my work exciting. But when I grew weary or disgruntled, like Emily Dickinson, I too tired of the world and sometimes found it lacking, the gentler joys of tea, sherry, and conversation with women friends, and I've made many good ones here, have always been a genuine pleasure. Thank you . . . and good-bye. (*The girls applaud Mrs. Plumm. Carter enters and brings in flowers. Muffy, Kate, Holly, Rita and Samantha watch as Mrs. Plumm exits with Carter and Susie Friend and Leilah who have gone up to congratulate her.*)

END SCENE

ACT TWO

SCENE 9

MAN'S VOICE FADING INTO WOMAN'S VOICE. A liberal arts college for women of talent is more important today than at any time in the history of her education. Women still encounter overwhelming obstacles to achievement and recognition despite gradual abolition of legal and political disabilities. Society has trained women from childhood to accept a limited set of options and restricted levels of aspirations.

SAMANTHA. I saw Carter's Wittgenstein movie on Public Television.

KATE. Maybe I should have married Carter.

MUFFET. Leilah got married in Iraq.

KATE. You're kidding.

MUFFET. She married some Iraqi journalist, archeologist. She gave up her citizenship and converted to Moslem. She can never be divorced.

RITA. Oh, my God.

KATE. Sometimes I thought I was a bad friend to Leilah and other times I just thought she was crazy. (*Rita touches Kate assuringly.*) Rita, how's your novel coming?

RITA. Kate, do you ever have anxiety attacks? I mean the kind that gives you the shits. I'm up every night till five A.M. and then I have fever dreams that I'm back in Cranfield Heights and my father has put me in the caboose of a Lionel train that goes through the Fundamentalist Church. And the men in the congregation are staring at my cunt singing, "Meow, Meow, Meow, Meow, Meow, Meow." Marilyn, my shrink says to start slowly. So I figure if I can sleep in the morning, watch a little tube at night, I'll have it together long enough to write my novel. I figure if I can make it to forty, I can be pretty fucking amazing.

KATE. I don't know, Rita. Maybe I don't have an artistic temperament, like you and Holly. I went to see a shrink this year. A friend of Kent's.

MUFFET. Who's Kent?

KATE. The man I was sort of living with. He started objecting to my working late. I guess it never occurred to me in college that someone wouldn't want me to be quite so uncommon. Anyway, I went to see this shrink and we had four productive sessions together and I feel fine.

MUFFET. Katie, you were all better after four sessions? You're still an over-achiever.

KATE. I don't live with Kent anymore. Kent's a lovely "enlightened" man who wants to marry Donna Reed. All right Donna Reed with an M.A. But I guess right now I'm committed to my work. (*Pause.*) Muffet do you really like insurance?

MUFFET. Wallace Stevens was in Insurance. When I first took my job I wondered what I was doing being an insurance seminar hostess. I mean, where was my prince? I guess I assumed something special would happen to me. Now I live in Hartford and I go to work every day and I won't be in the Alumnae Magazine like you, Katie, at the Justice Department or Nina Mandelbaum with her pediatric pulmonary specialist. But, I never thought I'd be supporting myself and I am. (*Kate touches Muffet's hand.*) Rita, I don't see how you can become strong living off Timmy. You're not doing anything.

RITA. We're suing Timmy's mother for his stocks. Actually, Kate, I was going to ask you about them—we need a good lawyer. The stocks are in his name, but in Timmy's mother's vault.

SAMANTHA. Rita, do you love Timmy?

RITA. I thought he'd be my Leonard Woolf. (*Pause.*) I just wanted to be protected like you, Samantha. (*Rita puts her arm around Samantha.*) Samantha, you have a good marriage, don't you?

SAMANTHA. Yes, I guess I do. Sometimes I get intimidated by all of Robert's friends who come to the house. And I think I haven't done very much of anything important. So I don't talk. But Robert respects me. (*She smiles. Pause.*) I don't want to sound like Mrs. Plumm, but I just want to say that I'm glad we all got together today. I had second thoughts about seeing all of you, especially Kate and Rita. Sometimes I think you might disapprove of what I do. I don't live alone, I'm not a professional and I tend to be too polite. What I really want to tell you is Robert and I are having a baby.

MUFFET. (*Gets up to kiss Samantha.*) That's wonderful, Samantha.

RITA. Why didn't you tell us?

SAMANTHA. It's not as easy as telling you I was getting married to him. Remember when I ran into the room? Now there are more options. I decided that I was a little embarrassed to tell you, but I'm also happy.

KATE. (*Kisses Samantha.*) I'm so pleased for you, Samantha, really. I even promise to sit for you on Election Day—that's my one day off. (*Pause.*) I wonder if I'll ever decide to have a child. I hardly think about it and when I do I tell myself there's still a lot of time. I wonder what it's like when you stop thinking there's a lot of time left to make changes. (*Pause. Samantha smiles slightly.*)

RITA. (*Trying to make conversation, and putting her arm around Samantha and Holly.*) I bought the new James Taylor album last week, I put it on at five A.M. and I thought this will be a comfort. It will remind me of my friends and I'll be able to make some connection between the past and the present. And all I heard was, "Carly, I love you, darling I do." Now, how did he turn out so well adjusted? Every other person I talk to is suddenly fine and has decided to go to medical school or has found inner peace through EST. I just had hoped that at least James Taylor would hold out for something more ambiguous.

HOLLY. (*Who has been listening intently during the scene.*) You know for the past six years I have been afraid to see any of you. Mostly because I haven't made any specific choices. My parents used to call me three times a week at seven A.M. to ask me, "Are you thin, are you married to a root canal man, are you a root canal man?" And I'd hang up and wonder how much longer am I going to be in "transition." I guess since college I've missed the comfort and acceptance I felt with all of you. And I thought you didn't need that anymore, so I didn't see you.

KATE. Holly, I don't want to go back and have "Gracious Living" and tea anymore. But I still want to see all of you. We knew we were natural resources before anyone decided to tap us. (*Pause for a moment as the girls all look at each other and finally smile together.*)

HOLLY. Let's have a toast.

SAMANTHA. All right, pumpkins, a toast, to Katie's law firm.

KATE. To Robert.

HOLLY. To Rita's novel.

MUFFET. To Wallace Stevens.

ALL. To Carter.

KATE. I'm glad we decided to get together today too. I've been feeling a little numb lately. And I know I wasn't like that in college. You remember a person, don't you? Anyway, lately, especially at those boring meetings, I look around at all those wing-tip feet and I remember Holly saying men write with their cocks— and I suspect many of the junior partners do, and Rita writing her novel, and Samantha being a closet wit, and Muffet and her prince. (*Pause.*) I'm glad we got together too. I miss you. (*Pause as she looks at all of them.*) And I've got to go. I'll get the check.

SAMANTHA. We could charge it to Robert.

KATE. No, I'll take it as a tax deduction. Holly, what are you doing?

HOLLY. I keep a list of options. Just from today's lunch, there's law, insurance, marry Leonard Woolf, have a baby, bird watch in Bolivia. A myriad of openings.

KATE. I've got to go. Kent says I dawdle. (*Pause.*) You all have my numbers. (*After Kate exits there is silence in the room. The girls look at each other quietly.*)

SAMANTHA. My dad was re-elected Mayor of Naperville.

HOLLY. My sister is marketing director of Proctor and Gamble.

RITA. Ada Grudder won the Nobel Prize. No, she didn't really, but I like to think so.

MUFFET. (*Getting up to put on her coat.*) Let's go to the movies.

SAMANTHA. (*Getting up.*) I have my car outside. Let's go see "Cries and Whispers."

MUFFET. (*Muffet laughs slightly and puts her arm around*

Samantha.) Hey, Holly, did you know Melissa Weex became a Rockette?

RITA. (*Moving to Holly, and putting on her coat.*) Timmy says when I get my head together, and if he gets the stocks, I'll be able to do a little writing. I think if I make it to forty I can be pretty amazing. (*She takes Holly's hand.*) Holly, when we're forty we can be pretty amazing. You too Muffy and Samantha, when we're (*Rita pauses for a moment.*) . . . forty-five we can be pretty fucking amazing. (*The Women exit with their arms around each other.*)

END

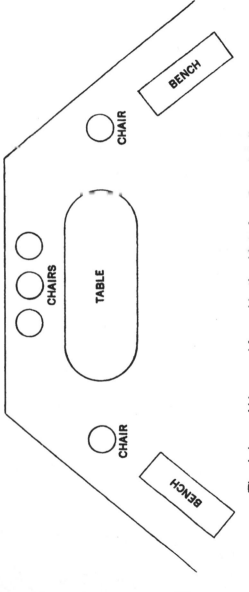

(The chairs would be moved forward by the girls to form the college living room. Benches would double as girls' beds.)

SCENE DESIGN

"UNCOMMON WOMEN AND OTHERS"

PROPERTY LIST

ACT ONE

Scene 1

Cigarettes and matches
Assorted drinks, on table

Scene 3

Tea service (cups, teapot, cream and sugar) on tray
Plate of finger sandwiches
Mayonnaise, on server
Jar of honey
Bottle of brandy, and glasses
Napkins
Plates
Silverware
Napkin box

Scene 4

College catalogue

Scene 5

Note (Susie)
Chocolates, in note

Scene 6

Book (Kate)

Scene 7

Diaphragm, and *Orthocreme* jelly

Scene 8

Bottle of sherry
Glasses
Record player
Package of "corn nuts" (Samantha)
Telephone
Glass (Mrs. Plumm)

Act Two

Scene 1

Pitch pipe

Scene 3

Make-up kit (Muffet)
Chocolate bunny } (Leilah)
Books

Scene 4

Jar of peanut butter
Jar of marshmallow fluff
Box of crackers

Scene 5

Hair brush (Samantha)
"Piglet" doll

Scene 6

Typewriter
Tape player

Scene 7

Pencil (Kate)
Telephone
Cigarettes & matches (Holly)
Raccoon coat

Scene 8

Tea service, on tray

Scene 9

Flowers (Carter)

NOTES
(Use this space to make notes for your production)

NOTES
(Use this space to make notes for your production)

NOTES

(Use this space to make notes for your production)

NOTES
(Use this space to make notes for your production)